contra / diction

by

Candace Simmons

1663 LIBERTY DRIVE, SUITE 200
BLOOMINGTON, INDIANA 47403
(800) 839-8640
www.authorhouse.com

First published by AuthorHouse 07/29/04

ISBN: 1-4184-2381-5 (e)
ISBN: 1-4184-2382-3 (sc)

Printed in the United States of America
Bloomington, Indiana

This book is printed on acid-free paper.

i want to apologize upfront for not being strong
for not being righteous
for not having the answers
for not being clever
for not caring how this sounds
for not caring if this moves
for daring to be myself and knowing
it's not genius
i'm lucky if it's poetic
and i'm blessed if it's truth
i just wanted to apologize up front

...Continuation...

i have been a part of so many systems in this life
i was born in a hospital
'we give you health and life and make a profit'

taught in a school
'we teach you ABC's, 123's, good manners, proper english,
and all that other good stuff...but get out of control or act
out the norm and we'll label you for the rest of your life,
and your parents will believe us'

and polished through higher education
'we are a training ground for future leaders, but if you
end up working at Popeye's after four years or more at this
fine institution don't tell anybody you went here'

systems are beautiful, no?...show us which way to go...
who to be & how to act...well, since I know the rules I can
break them, right? I can Choose to take my own path now.
and no i'm not rebelling...i'm simply living.

and still afraid…knowing heroes are often more fearful than cowards.

gotta understand both sides to appreciate
each mission
open your eyes to read in between the lines of
contradiction

EXCUSE ME FOR MY LACK OF STRUCTURE
EXCUSE ME IF MY RHYMS LACK-LUSTURE
I'M JUST A SCATTERED WRITER
I'M NOT A FREEDOM FIGHTER
I'M NOT A POET LAUREATTE

some just like the way i spit/or write /or kick some spoken
word
(sike that's a lie) cause i rarely recite/just jot it on pieces
of paper/
and occasionally type it

i've been known to make noise cease and mutes speak
excuse me for my bluntness I figure no one likes sugar-
coated shit
so i've decided to spit fire turning my desire for mental
masturbation
into fetus fallacies gestating (sorry for the side note)
but i've said bye-bye to humble pie and decided to really
gloat
matta-a-fak i sang so many praises upon myself my best
friend decided to cut my throat
i'll never be afraid of speech
who might i reach with mere words you ask?
why child this is just an introductory class
you'll start to see the masses sway and move next session
Thank you all,
This concludes my daily lesson
(CLAPS)

who knew written word would go out of style
before it was popular
had to change my style
my voice
and my clothes
just to get on the mic
and spit something
i'd rather just write
all this hype for someone as shy as myself
wish i could let this Movement pass me by…
this is obviously a cry for help
speak write-no…speak well

i must confess i've been blessed by your agony
reborn in it
baptized in your tears
years of suffering
your pain equals my fuel?
no…i just need to be rescued
also you
tonight
Sundown
and Saved

i made it just barely
just barely i failed
it took but only minutes
my breath i held…
i opened it slowly
the Truth it told me i closed it and continued my day
with new grief
with new know…ledge

i could never understand what was so different about me
and my life
until i really got to know others
Listening
hearing them speak
seeing their moments of weakness and shame
we all get kicked at some point
we're all in this together (despite what some may think)
yet we're so separate everything seems to be happening to
only us

open your eyes and ears
learn from those that appear unfamiliar…
by your lungs i breathe

i feel so peaceful
now that i'm not rushing
everything that will be will be
and i'm writing and will write
even if i never get published
because i must
and that's just the way it is

praying to yourGod for me
don't know how to defend my faith
or my doubt (so i won't)
i doubt that me beliefs have anything to do with you (you
whole heartily believe otherwise)
pray for us

wow i'm hurting
damn i'm numb
wondering what's this life for
and will someone come
and rescue me
yes i do mean rescue
and i don't want to offend any feminist
but i need a man to do this job
i was told that one would come
i'm becoming desperately impatient
as i wait for direction
it's not affection i yearn for
but the inception
of a new way of living

i know everyone favors consistency
but since i'm consistently schizo i will change tenses from
time to time
I WILL SWITCH between upper and LOWER case
i will be a disgrace to all inglish teachers and gramma
preachers
to all editors...i love editors. i play one in real life
for this i offer no apology
but my sincerest get over it

I don't feel any certain thing...
write now

I was born by the river…
i was born from a quiver
i was birthed for a purpose
i'm making my way along
how i hate poems that are I, I, I
why do i hate people that never say goodbye?
why do I always become exactly what i despise?
***

instant gratification is
like scratching mosquito bites it
can leave marks
***

Dear Lord,
no more complaining
no more doubting
no more lying to myself
no more fakin' the funk
no more juggling between wisdom and knowledge
acting so ignorant
trying to portray innocence
no more holding back
please God can you grant me that?
i'll take one at a time, i'll start with lying…
because i'm starting to feel something's not right with this
I need you now. Amen.

getting angrier by the second
do you take me for a fool
cause i take you for the worst kind of person
a punk that doesn't know of his punknisity
you dress it up well
but believe me it smells
i won't tell of your secret
no not yet
but i bet you before it's all over you will HAVE NOTHING
LEFT

She's still fuming
She's still confused
Now I know how it feels to feel completely
USED

i'm caught between wanting to say everything and
wanting to say nothing
wondering if this world will out weight gravity
this is not the opportune time
but the only time
cause the longer i wait the worse it will get
and pretty soon there will be no more ink to paper
just tears and years and spit on these pages

there's so much world to see
but you gotta 'pay your dues'
sometimes a lifetime
before you can even leave the country (if you ever do)

some kids never leave their block
some adults never stop to think

Mind/travel begins the trip
complacency
Ends it

she's dying to live

I'm in the middle
I go to class in between
I've seen things below the water
and at the top
they can't hear me scream

I woke up this morning with ink on my fingertips...
        ???
Has my identity been stolen...or did my family catch me
Praying to the East?

making something out of nothing
that's what you tell me...I'm trippin'
actually I am clumsy
but my mind is free…
I seen what I seen and you ain't who you said you be

"take me where the darkness is still beautiful"
                            CEE-LO

take me to this place original home black lakes and stars
tears hit brick walls
my spirit falls and so remembrance is near
before email, stock crashes & implants
there were ashes

breathing now
like fire and sky
so powerful and high

without anything else
but existence
there's remembrance

the night was still sacred before we raped it
and made it full of fear

Everyone sees me sunny side up
sometimes hard to know what's going on
deep in my gut
guess I'm still trying to see
what's really there
if I were strip bear from my clothes to my soul
I wonder what would reflect
don't really care whose looking anymore
what angle would you like
i'll turn to my right...it reflects the best
Light...
I was simply broken
not shattered
so the past doesn't matter
I'm moving forward as the smokes clears
this feels so weird
my pain dissipates as I wait for answers with open ears...
if I looked like you and spoke like you
would you hear me then
what's the Truth to many
belies the rest
so I attempt to test the waters of pure Honesty

naps and cries
straightening lies

sometimes my words get stuck in numbness
sometimes I yearn for oneness
with another
sometimes i wish i was brave enough to uncover
myself
but unfortunately
I'm part queen of the jungle...
½ cowardly lion

some writers think they can only write with words
speak with mouths
but they've forgotten
(or never quite knew)

tears fall upon dirty shoes
mud covers faces
hands clap
and knees raise like Bob praising the Almighty

think I got that feelin'

Thought maybe music was dead…then the Ave I heard

So this prayer I said…
"Thank You Jesus" (in 31 languages)

keep spreading Truth to the people breaking chains with
soulful melodies knowing that you were planting seeds
before CDs and way before open mic

when you turn around and see your following
turn to God before you lead
and when it all seems so wonderful
be thankful for the blessings
if you start losing faith in the purpose
look deeper for the lesson

Shining Stars that's who you be
your music…your message
allows others to breathe
more easily

Thank you,
for the Healing. peace

read the books…searched for truth hated ones that
brought my ancestors here and still i looked for knowledge
left no stone unturned felt a void in my life and many
lessons I learned was enlightened then realized I'm not the
only one searching
the authors the speakers and the ones who hold the
masses the workshops with the prophets selling pipe
dreams it's not all about schemes see some actually believe
in what they preach but there's not enough ambiguity too
much explained and if they got all the answers why are
we in the same game trying to figure out the same thing
not trying to be clear cause I don't want to give names
placing blame won't solve the problem cause there's
always those that try and hustle peace and truth…we
are a great people but this world is bigger than the flesh
more than who's best got the most money can say the right
things and know the right verses

let no one lead you astray not even yourself.

we get wrapped up in people, especially ourselves,

do you really think one amongst us will be the savior? do you think

ignoring this reality is doing yourself a favor?

I wish for peace but wouldn't know her if we met
"Hi, I'm peace"
yeah okay, scuz me, you in my way
I'm going places meeting people trying new foods

gotta be multifaceted
multitask it
multi-face kid
to survive today
one thing at a time, one person, one way
just don't cut it
you gotta sell your soul
and buy it back
then divide it
get more and profit
sell it again and again
burn a few copies
and let everybody cop it

chorus : tried to swallow life whole
nearly chocked on my soul
l looked death in it's eyes
didn't realize
just couldn't understand what was happening to me
couldn't even think or eat
didn't sleep, barely blinked
the things I've seen you wouldn't believe
the devil had a hold on me

i already knew
i've always known that you and i would die
it was unhealthy but it helped me
corrected my vision
made me appreciate sanity
made me appreciate solitude
we
we were unhealthy
but it healed me
no thanks to you
but I thank you

taking this papyrus & ink
stopping my silence isn't always golden
did you think you'd stolen my last words
i won't be the only one hurt
vengeance
isn't mine
but karma is real
call it what you want one day you'll feel what i felt
tell me to accept the cards
i've been dealt
tell me the deck is on my side all i have to do is cut
you some slack
slide 5 my way
i'll never even look down
or back
just take my hand
turn my cards to you
all Queens
and walk away from this game
Peacefully
with my army behind me

i'm not conscious
i'm just awake
i'm not natural
i'm just not fake
i wear a head-wrap when my hair is tore up
i'm not elevated
i'm just growing up

she's such the afro-centric queen she say things like
"overstand" and "pass that green"

what a lyrical genius, such a stylish gent…

called myself checking out his last album
simply too hot to hold so i watched as blackness melted
into the floor
slid my toes into the charcoaled sand closed my eyes and
listened to that fire crackle
contemplating every line
smiling at the clever delivery
nodding my head to the beats
infectious
remembering all the times i banned this music from my
car
shaking my head in disgust at every new single
i was wrong and right…he was wrong and right
i guess life is made up of
 moments of clarity
small moments that barely peak through
but when they do
it hits hard
my muscles tense in anticipation
relaxed
silence
my body…numb and shivering
tears streamed down my face
looking at the picture of Pac on my right wall
then down at the soul rebel/mystical brother
collecting dust by the side of my bed
turned off the stereo
shook the stress from my neck
and prayed

get your freak on!...
while you're at it get your drink on
go 'head girl you grown girl

(sounds kinda silly when it's in print)

add a few more lines and a bangin' beat and we all doing
the happy feet

what's so great about taking notes
what's so great about remembering quotes
why should i have to read books that never mention
my people's contributions
all my people
African
no matter how hard i look
i think i'm losing my mind
and i can't blame her at times for running away

why is he talking so much
why is my brain walking away…please stay
I know you're tired
tired of taking notes
tired of retaining information
tired of being ignored sick of facts
i figure we can run away together
cause my body's tired too back aching getting migraines
skin feeling all funny in these adult clothes
i don't want to grow old if it's this boring
i don't want to get big if it requires conforming
he's still talking
doesn't he realize my day was long and this night class is
running too late
is it so wrong that my mind just wants to rest and my body
wants to play
come back brain…i said COME BACK
I promise…
not to let you turn into mush
not to burn you like a bush
not to smoke you like a weed
just come back brain
come back
please

something amazing might happen tomorrow
can't wait until sunrise & good news

Wish I could write this with the point of a star...wouldn't go so far as to say this is magical, but my hand is hot like Jupiter...the air is getting thinner...but wait-will you come with me on this galaxy trip?

See what we have is unearthly...too much for land and water, trees become fearful as our minds eclipse...lips do more than kiss but create new life on planets undiscovered. I want to uncover myself standing before you like Venus, watching you rise. Manhood knocking down nations built on lies as your tongue touches my flesh I began to flow like rivers. Legs part with knowing and rain begins to fall as we cease to exist in this form. I've always known of this...
Consummation

kissed your eyelids while you slept
massaged your hands
ran my fingers over your scalp
you smiled (must think your dreaming)
turned on the humidifier
so your breathing would calm
and turned the radio down
it's called the "quiet storm"

in the morning you rubbed your eyes
scratched your butt
and asked me what's for breakfast
kissing my cheek with your offensive breath

laughing to myself…good morning love

I love you more and more everyday
I never thought I'd say that about anyone but I do
as Ms. Badu said, 'you reflect the light of the Sun'
and you do it so innocently
you don't even realize how your light shines
how your smile heals
when I'm with you
I think of the love poems that I said I would never write
I wanted to rebel against this feeling
but it's so much bigger and badder than I'll ever be
I must submit
I have to admit that I love you
more and more everyday
and when I'm with you I say things I thought I'd never say
like I miss you when you're gone
why do you have to go
and all other 'caring phrases'
I'm so new to this that I can't even explain it
though I've said these things before
and read a similar script I never really
played myself in any of those roles
I was a stunt double
falling in and out of situations I wish I'd
never stepped inside the scene
and don't ask me why I went from loving you to movies
you make me do silly things
like taking metaphors too far
I'm in2deep too ever come out
and I'm not complaining
because I love this feeling
but even more
I love you

I found out I loved you like I found out I was black
I just looked in the mirror and saw my skin
different
beautiful and glowing
I knew something was hmmm...peculiar, just like I knew I
was a girl
everything seemed extra and not the same
I can't understand why you look at me as you do
I never really figured out who loved who first

do I confuse you as much as I confuse myself
what do I do with the rest of my time?

I've loved and am loved by you
what's next

becoming afraid of my imagination
it's becoming too vivid
i see you coming towards me
we are one image
these visions are losing me, plastered
with light…if you could see them would they match your
dreams
would the images blow your mind
will this be my Final Fantasy
will you come quietly with me

you said you weren't ready for the responsibility and
commitment
of a 'real relationship'...couldn't take it
couldn't make time for phone calls and visits
you spoke and spoke about how this is all new to you
and I listened
repented for my feelings
luckily you can't hear my thoughts like I hear yours
please, from now on say what you really mean
instead of calling me queen
speak what you feel
call me fool
say you want to me naked and silent

i hear you thoughts
watch your gestures
CLEARLY you've got the wrong one

will you please kiss
your last taste of this sweet naivety

wish you were here
to get the rest of your belongings

want so badly to hear your voice
without hearing your lies

why was I trying so hard to do the right things
saying all the nice things
and ALWAYS smiling

every week
dress got tighter
teeth whiter
hair straighter
still SMILING

a few heads turn
but no one from your crew
and especially not you

mirror mirror on the wall...
why you let me go out there like that?

I ain't do a thing girlfriend
but reflect
keep all opinions to myself
you don't pay me enough attention for that
got windex?...please use now
clean me girl
clean me good

never smiled
in a mirror
only cried in a mirror
hope one day blemishes disappear
year after year I'm more comfortable with me
but I still fear what I see
wish this glass would break
and change my fate
7 more years of a life I can't take
wait...someone's opening the door
I see a face
in shock
as the bottle drops to the floor
40 pills or more scatter the floor
my tears fall
why can't I crawl under the earth?
looking at her reflection
and wonder why she even gave birth
to what I see before me

God make me stronger
don't know how much longer I can take
everyone staring
asking questions
and assuming
I wish it wasn't me
seems like so much burden to bear
got the answers burning inside
but who can I trust?

we stay cloaked
in hot lies
letting family ties choke throats
sick of singing
this song
the devil wrote

when i feel like this i wanna smoke a cigarette and i don't
even smoke
it's just not supposed to be this way…all the let downs and
disappointments
the people and their promises…always broken

but wait there are others…

there are women that get their fingers chopped off for
being able to write
some mother somewhere can't sleep tonight because
she knows by next sunset her daughter won't feel whole
anymore and they will finally be sisters in suffering
confused as to why her genitalia is being mutilated, sewed
together or her clitoris removed
somewhere there's a little girl being used as an ashtray
because daddy's too drunk to know that she will never be
the same and some marks never fade
somehow somewhere a women has been killed for being
raped and bringing shame upon her family
and here on freedom's soil a victim of sexual assault is
being blamed for wearing a short skirt and having large
breast…because apparently some victims are not victims
at all

so tonight i will not get caught up in my blessings i
call problems because these women need me to stay
strong…because i will speak up and i will fight. but right
now i will light a candle for the women…hold on & keep
burning

What is my passion? What is my purpose?
How will I suffer?
should i just wait and see what happens
will laziness change my fate
because some people i know are not happy with where
they are
but they're content and that just doesn't make much sense
satisfied but not satiated…it's real crazy
and i've played this part so i know it well

babies and children with moms…both parents in prison.
entire families hungry. streets bleak and gray that just
need some serious clean-up, paint, and prayer. a 30 year
old that reads at a 1st grade level. people, entire families
hungry (it needs to be repeated). adults so stuck in their
past that they have low expectations for the youth. a young
black male that's more familiar with dc courts than a
college campus. black woman with a gun to her head too
afraid to ask for help, cause black folks not crazy, and we
definitely don't commit suicide.

this is suicide. suicide of a dream. suicide of a people. we
are killing ourselves.

encased in apathy and fear. from sad to upset to enraged
and then finally…numbness. gun to the temple of the
future.

"the way things have always been"…no

"but what can I do?"…start with love. end with love. this
is the purpose…now interpret

Been taken advantage of in so many ways…been abused
but in the end they will pay…been abandoned but didn't
need them anyway…been a liar and a thief and much
more…this is not a victims song…been a trader and a
cheat…been syrupy and sweet like a dream deferred…
been witness to countless wrongs, then acted like a
coward…been to hell and back, holding hands with the
devil.
tried to take my life. twice. but God wouldn't let me.
been a teacher. a student (can't live without learning)
been natural (my hair that is)…then put another perm in
been straight carried by niggas with "potential"
tried to stop saying "niggas" but the truth is consequential
the word is so significant
His Word is so magnificent (even when i don't Listen)

the U.S. is in a deficit but who really cares…long as we
look rich…think rich…the hell with the infrastructure.
could you imagine if America was a "third world" country
and even the Hilton sisters were hungry
what if the least of our worries was janet's boob and we
were literally starving…living without food…and we were
literally dying of HIV, what if AIDS were killing 1,000 a
day…oh wait it is.
but we protect out material possessions more than we
protect our bodies
need to cement a condom in the walk of fame for saving
so many lives
when used correctly
and saving so many lives cause most of us ain't ready to
cultivate a mind
and feed another mouth

wanted to be more outspoken all my life but i'm
wondering what's the point if no one's really listening. my
bling-bling don't shine but my heart is glistenin'
wish i didn't have to type these words but my hand
writing is illegible
would be nice just to cut and paste my thoughts and staple
them

sell them on the corner. with some incense and bottled
water

As I put my faith in an "invisible" God,
I automatically take away power from that which I do see.

so i'm taking a stroll naked removing masks bearing my
soul
only the Lord knows what the future may hold
as real as the Sun suspended in the air…
i wash away my cares
head back
eyes closed
feet in soil
dreamin' of a different reality

About the Author

Candace Simmons, who has been writing poetry and short stories since the age of 10, is making her publishing debut with this collection of poetry. She resides in Prince George's County, Maryland. Candace is a student at Bowie State University (an Historically Black University in Bowie, Md.) receiving her Bachelor's in Social Work.